ALL ABOUT ME

Reproducible Activity Sheets to Develop Self-Awareness, Self-Concept, and Life Skills in Your Students

Susanna Palomares

INNERCHOICE Publishing

15079 Oak Chase Court
Wellington, FL 33414

www.InnerchoicePublishing.com

edited by Dianne Schilling

illustrated by Roger Johnson

Copyright © 1991 by Innerchoice Publishing • All rights reserved
(Revised Edition, 2009)

ISBN - 10: 1-56499-058-7

ISBN - 13: 978-1-56499-058-7

INNERCHOICE Publishing
15079 Oak Chase Court
Wellington, FL 33414

www.InnerchoicePublishing.com

CONTENTS

Belonging

Purpose and Competence

Introduction

All About Me is a creative collection of 88 fun activity pages that help children develop accurate self-concepts, identify unique qualities and abilities, discover strengths, explore interests and learn about feelings. Each engaging, reproducible activity sheet encourages creativity and self-expression, and teaches important life skills while raising self-awareness and self-esteem.

Write On

Self-awareness and self-esteem are critical areas in the development of social-emotional learning. Children who understand and feel good about themselves are generally capable of higher performance and achievement in all areas. While there are many ways to facilitate the development of authentic self-awareness and healthy self-esteem, the activities in this book couple the process of self-examination with the tool of writing. Each exercise consists of one or more writing prompts that encourage the child to probe particular areas of memory and self-knowledge. Taken together, the exercises cover a wide range of experiences, beliefs, abilities and concerns, allowing students the opportunity to conceptualize and express many dimensions of themselves.

Because writing is structured and systematic, follows specific rules and requires students to organize, integrate and analyze their thoughts, the emotional and intellectual benefits of writing are often more meaningful to learning and self-development than simply thinking or fantasizing. The act of writing helps thoughts come together in a coherent manner, allowing students to capture insights, find meaning and grow in self-awareness.

Use Flexibly

Each reproducible page can be used alone or enlisted as a supplement to other strategies you are currently using. The pages are organized around four major building blocks of self-esteem and personal development: Identity, Belonging, Purpose and Competence.

The important life skills of problem solving, decision making, and goal setting are given special attention in the section on Purpose and Competence, each through a series of sequential activity sheets. After the entire class has completed these sheets, encourage individual students to follow the suggested steps whenever they are dealing with a situation in which a formal process might enhance their efforts to solve a problem, make a decision, or work toward a goal. Repeated use will reinforce these critical capabilities where they count most—in the real world—and will greatly enhance your students' feelings of self-worth and self-esteem.

Extend the Learning

The elements of encouraging interaction, generating discussion, creating spin-off assignments, and making connections that are built into *All About Me* will help students extend their learning.

Encourage Interaction.

Socializing is an important activity for children and a critical aspect of learning. Furthermore, developing positive peer-group relations is a primary task of childhood. So, as much as possible, encourage discussion and sharing. For example, after the students have completed their activity sheets, ask them to get together in two's, three's or small groups to discuss what they have written.

Generate Discussion.

After the students have completed an activity sheet, pull the entire group together and ask questions related to the topic of the activity. Use student responses as springboards to discussion and additional sharing.

Create Spin-off Assignments.

If students show particular interest in a topic, suggest that they create their own unique activity sheets for others to complete. You may find yourself developing new activity sheets as well. Be open to ongoing creative collaboration as you and the children delve with increasing enthusiasm into the subject of "me."

Make Connections.

The feelings, thoughts and behaviors associated with subjects like friendship, thankfulness, creativity, talents, rules and positive thinking are so thoroughly woven into the fabric of everyday life, you should have no difficulty relating them to what is happening to the students, both academically and interpersonally. Make as many connections as you possibly can; they will enrich school life and add relevancy and immediacy to the activities.

Respect Student Privacy

Never require the students to share what they have written if they don't want to. When you invite sharing, make it clear that the students may offer as little or as much information as they like—including none at all. What they share and how completely they share it is up to them. All About Me activity sheets are designed first and foremost to encourage introspection and self-awareness. Sharing and interaction are secondary benefits, but should never be forced. Although the activity sheets do not probe highly sensitive areas, students will occasionally write something that they prefer to keep confidential. Honor that desire.

Reproducible Activity Pages

I'm Glad I'm Me!

No one looks the way I do,
I have noticed that it's true:
No one walks the way I walk.
No one talks the way I talk.
No one plays the way I play.
No one says the things I say.
 I'm special,
 I am Me!
There's no one
I would rather be!

Things about me that I like and appreciate:

1. _____

2. _____

3. _____

4. _____

5. _____

6. _____

All About Me

My name is _____

I was born on _____ at _____ **a.m.**
p.m.

I have _____ eyes and _____ hair, and I

     weigh _____ pounds.

Something I really like to do is _____

_____

The thing I like best about school is _____

_____

The thing I like least about school is _____

_____

My favorite food is _____

My favorite TV show is _____

The things I want in a friend are _____

_____

The thing that makes me a good friend is _____

_____

Something I do well is _____

_____

I feel happy when _____

I feel sad when _____

I feel scared when _____

If I could have one wish, it would be _____

_____

MY BIRTHDAY

How old will you be
on your next birthday? _____

Draw a candle on the cake for each year,
the first candle has already been drawn.

Who would you invite to your birthday party?

_____   _____
_____   _____
_____   _____
_____   _____
_____   _____
_____   _____
_____   _____

Make a list of what you want for your birthday.

_____   _____
_____   _____
_____   _____
_____   _____
_____   _____
_____   _____
_____   _____

The Keys to Happiness

Interview two people. Discover **three** important things that bring happiness to each of them.

Name: _____

1. _____

2. _____

3. _____

Name: _____

1. _____

2. _____

3. _____

Now, take some time to think about what makes you happy. What are the keys to your happiness? Write what they are on the keys.

Flying HIGH

There are many ways that you can help yourself to feel good. Things you do, places you go, and what you think about are just some of the ways you might help yourself to be happy. Write about the different things you do to make yourself feel good and be happy on the spaces below.

What's Important to YOU?

Pretend you're going on a trip around the world, and you will be gone for a year. Besides your clothes, you can only take five things with you. Think about the five most important things that you would want to take with you, and list them in the suitcase.

1. _____

2. _____

3. _____

4. _____

5. _____

The Time of My Life

I was born

   on _____

Today's date

   is _____

MY PAST	MY FUTURE
_____	_____
_____	_____
_____	_____
_____	_____
_____	_____
_____	_____
_____	_____
_____	_____
_____	_____

This is a time line of your life. Write in the date you were born and today's date. How many years have passed since you were born? _____. How many months? _____. How many days? _____. Does that seem like a long time? Think about important events in your life. Places you've been, accomplishments you've achieved, and things you've learned. Write about some of these things on the lines provided under the heading "My Past." Now think about your future. What are some things you'd like to do and accomplish in your life. Write about those things on the lines provided under the heading "My Future."

Something I'm Good At

Everyone has strengths and weaknesses. When we aren't so good at something, we can work at improving ourselves. When we are good at something, we can recognize our ability and feel proud about it. Think about something you are good at. Maybe you're a good friend, or maybe you're good at reading or math. It could be a sport, music, art, or anything.

Something I am very good at is _____

_____

_____

_____

_____

I learned this by _____

_____

_____

_____

_____

If I were going to teach this to someone else, this is how I would do it: _____

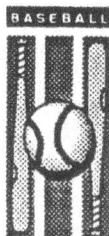

_____

_____

_____

_____

How I Spend My Time

Look at the four categories below, and think about how you spend your time with each one.

Fill up each square with the activities you do in each category.

School	Home
Sports and Hobbies	Friends

Talented Me

What talent or special ability would you like to develop? Write a description of the talented you here: _____

_____

Very few talented people are just "discovered." They work hard to develop their talents and abilities. If you want the world to know about your talent, you have to:

• Develop it! How? _____

_____

• Practice it! Where? _____

_____

• Show it off! To whom? _____

_____

• Ask people to help you! Who? _____

_____

On the back side of this sheet draw a picture of yourself expressing your talent. ➤

Do you know the names of 2 successful people who have this kind of talent? Who are they?

1._____   2. _____

Describe what you will do in the next month to start developing <u>your</u> talent.

BY _____ , I WILL _____
     (Date)

_____

_____

_____

A Poem About Me

There is a special kind of 5 line poem called a cinquain. Here's how to use the format to write a poem about yourself:

    1st line—   one word—your first name

    2nd line—   two words—adjectives that describe you

    3rd line—   three words—action words that end in "ing"

    4th line—   four words—a phrase that describes you

    5th line—   one word—noun, another name for you

Here are some examples:

Sandy	**David**
Funny, friendly	**Intelligent, creative**
Laughing, talking, sharing	**Working, helping, caring**
Always enjoys being herself	**Gets everything done well**
Friend	**Student**

Write a poem about yourself using the cinquain format. Put your name on line 1.

1. _____

2. _____

3. _____

4. _____

5. _____

Now write a poem about a friend.

1. _____

2. _____

3. _____

4. _____

5. _____

I AM . . . *POETRY*

In large letters print each letter of your first name from top to bottom in the space below. For each letter, think of a word beginning with the same letter that describes you. For example, if your name were Chris you might write the following:

C = <u>C</u>alm

H = <u>H</u>appy

R = <u>R</u>edhead

I = <u>I</u>ndependent

S = <u>S</u>illy sometimes

Now write a paragraph about yourself using as many of the same words as you can.

_____

_____

_____

_____

FEELINGS Are OK!

You are never good or bad because of the way you feel. Finish these sentences to tune in to your feelings.

1. This morning, when I got up, I felt _____

2. I feel amused when _____
   _____

3. Walking in mud with my bare feet makes me feel
   _____

4. I felt angry once when _____
   _____

5. _____ makes me feel scared.

6. Red makes me feel _____

7. On a windy day, I feel _____

8. It is _____
   to talk about feelings.

9. I feel small when _____

10. _____ makes me feel soft and cuddly.

11. The last time I was surprised was when _____
    _____

12. The color that makes me the happiest is _____

13. _____ is how I feel about Math.

14. _____ makes me feel big.

15. Stars make me feel _____

Feeling Faces

Draw faces that show the emotion for each of the feeling words below.

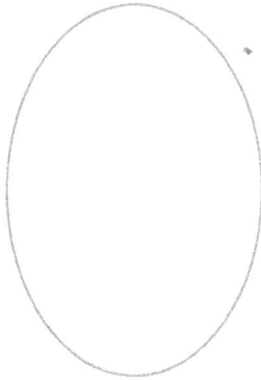

Sad

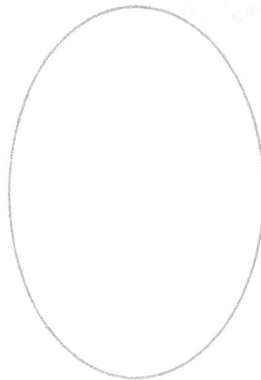

Angry

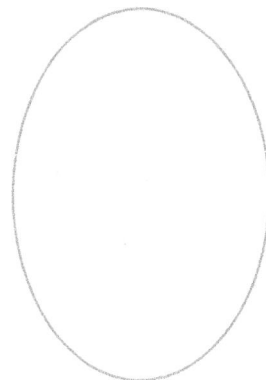

Happy

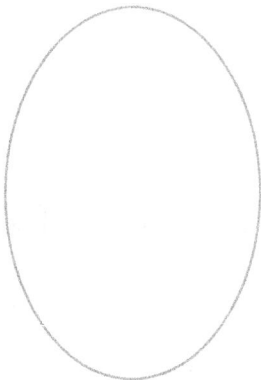

Scared

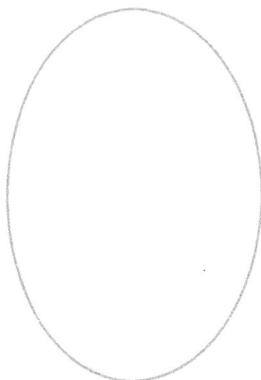

Confused

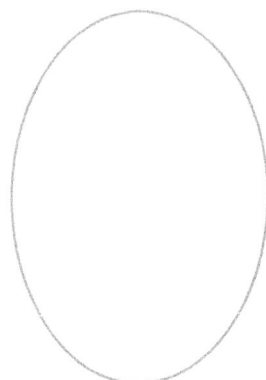

Surprised

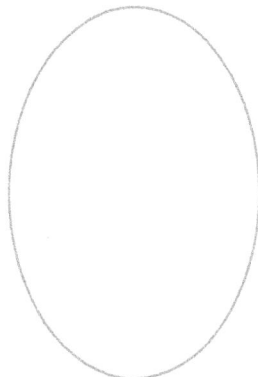

Joyful

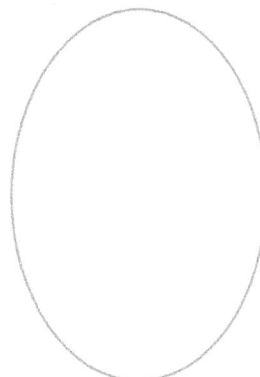

Excited

Here's a tip: Imagine having the feeling yourself and then what your face looks like in a mirror or to others.

20

Take Responsibility for Your Feelings!

We all have situations and conditions in our lives that we feel negatively about. Think about a situation or condition in your life right now (or in the past) that causes you to feel anger, disappointment, embarrassment, sadness, or some other negative feeling. Write about the situation here. Describe what is going on and how you feel about it.

_____

_____

_____

_____

_____

_____

_____

Now, take responsibility for your thoughts by changing them. What other thoughts could you have about this situation that would help you to feel better? Be understanding with yourself, but be honest, too. (If you need more room, use the back of this sheet.)

_____

_____

_____

_____

_____

_____

_____

This Is Me: INSIDE and OUTSIDE

Think about who you are. How do other people see you? When your friends and family and teachers get to know you, what are you like to them? This is you on the outside. Now think about how you seem to yourself. This is you on the inside.

Pretend that the person in the illustration below is you. On the outside, write down all the words and sentences that describe how other people see you. On the inside, write the words and sentences that describe how you see yourself.

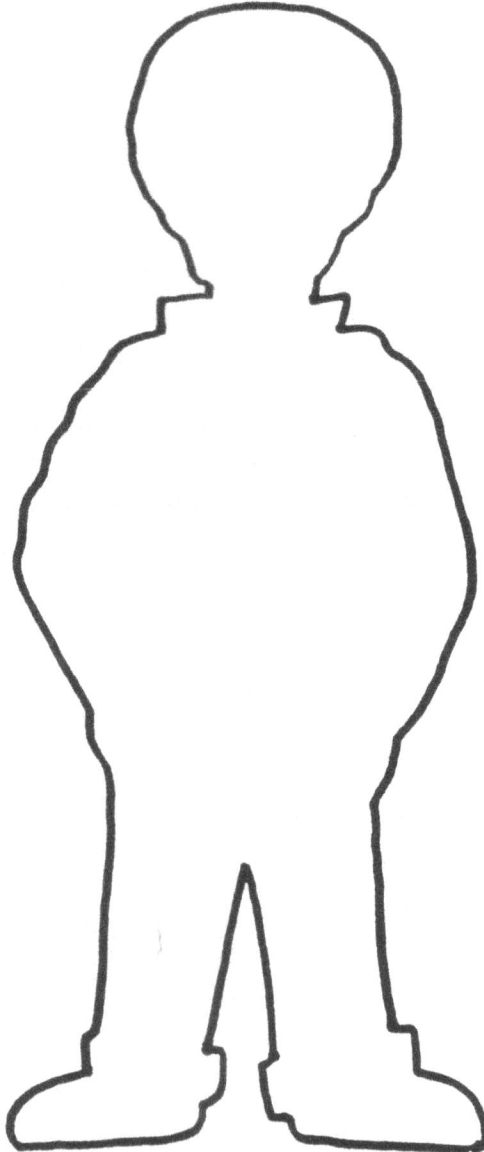

What's In Your Name?

Write your full name, including your first, middle , and last names.

First Name _____

Middle Name _____

Last Name _____

How many words can you make using only the letters in your name?

Now write all the words you can think of that rhyme with your first name:

...that rhyme with your middle name:

...that rhyme with your last name:

Looking INSIDE

What are the most important things in the world to you? Have you ever thought about that question?   What do you want most in life? Think about each of the questions below and then write your answers on the lines:

1. What kind of work do I want to do when I grow up?

   _____

2. Where would I like to live when I grow up?

   _____

3. What is one very important wish I have for myself?

   _____

4. What do I wish for the world?

   _____

5. If I could change one thing in the world, what would I change?

   _____

These Are a Few of My Favorite Things

Part of what makes you YOU are the things you like and don't like. Go through this activity and write about the things you like and don't like.

My favorite—

Musical group: _____

Holiday: _____

Restaurant: _____

T.V. show: _____

Comic/cartoon: _____

Amusement park: _____

Movie: _____

Song: _____

Food: _____

Other things I like: _____

What are some things that bother you and you don't like.

_____

_____

Answer these statements:

I really like it when _____

_____

I really don't like it when _____

_____

MY INTEREST TREE

Everybody has interests and talents. Think about some things that you are interested in. On each of the four major branches, write down the name of an activity or subject that interests you. For example, things like cooking, reading, sports, horseback riding, music, or animals. Then, in the spaces along and at the ends of the branches, draw pictures of some of the things involved with your area of interest. For example, if you write animals on a branch, you might draw pictures of a dog, a cat, and a rabbit in the spaces around the branch.

A Treasured Possession

Treasures are things that we value a great deal. Think about something that you treasure very much. Write about your treasured possession. Write about when you got your treasure, how you got it, what you do with it, and the reasons it is so important to you. If you run out of room, use the back of this paper.

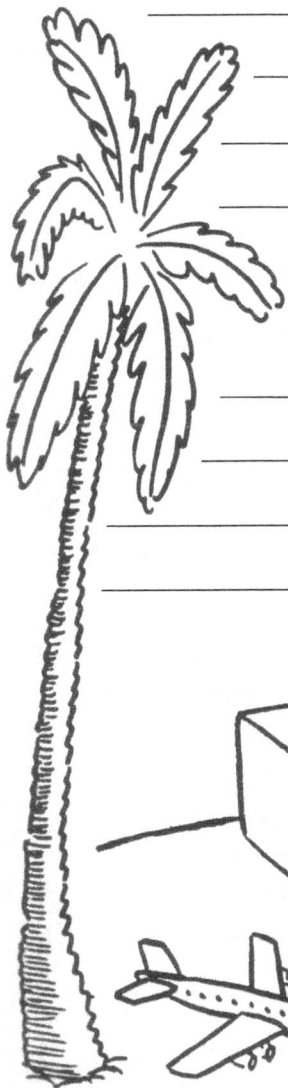

_____

_____

_____

_____

_____

_____

_____

_____

_____

10 Important Things in My Life

Think of 10 different things in your life that are very important to you. These can be people, pets, or possessions.

Write down and/or draw a different important item in each box.

1.	2.	3.
4.	5.	6.
7.	8.	10.
	9.	

MY ROOM

Think about your bedroom at home. Picture all the special things you have in your room. List as many of those things as you can think of:

_____   _____   _____

_____   _____   _____

_____   _____   _____

_____   _____   _____

_____   _____   _____

If you were going away and could only take 3 of your special possessions with you, which ones would you take?

1._____   2._____   3._____

Why did you choose these things?

_____

_____

_____

The BOOKS I've Enjoyed

Reading is a great activity. We can learn many things from books and we can spend many enjoyable hours reading.

Use this sheet to list the books you would like to read and to keep track of the books you've already read and enjoyed.

BOOKS I've read and enjoyed...

Title _____

Author _____

What the book is about: _____

_____

_____

Title _____

Author _____

What the book is about: _____

_____

_____

Title _____

Author _____

What the book is about: _____

_____

_____

Go to the next page to continue your list—

Title _____

Author _____

What the book is about: _____

_____

Title _____

Author _____

What the book is about: _____

_____

BOOKS I'd like to read...

Title _____

Author _____

Title _____

Author _____

Title _____

Author _____

Title _____

Author _____

If you want to add more books, use another paper. Always write down both the title and the author.

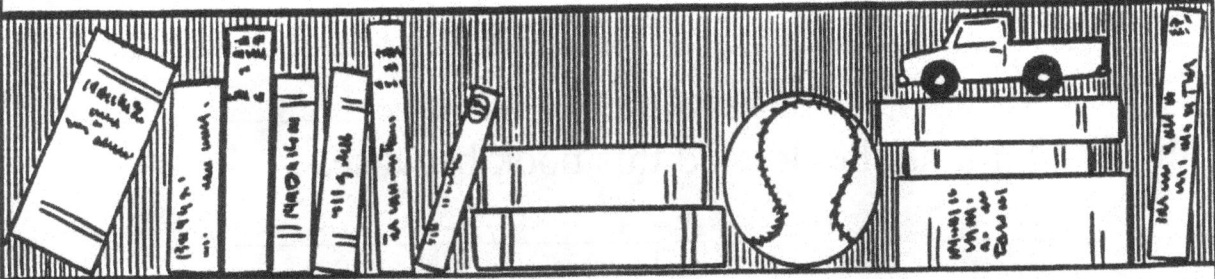

My FAVORITE Book!

Is there a particular book that you really enjoy? On the lines below write about this special book.

My favorite book is about:

_____

_____

The main characters in the book are:

_____

_____

The character I like best is _____,
and I like him or her because:

_____

_____

I think other kids should read this book because:

_____

_____

What Does It Mean?

A proverb is a short, often used saying that expresses a recognized truth or fact. Listed below are several well-known proverbs. Next to each one write what you think it means—

* **Do not put off until tomorrow what can be done today**

_____

_____

* **When life gives you a lemon, make lemonade**

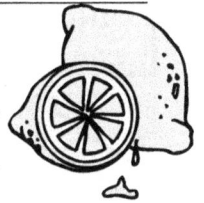

_____

_____

* **All that glitters is not gold**

_____

_____

* **Don't let the grass grow under your feet**

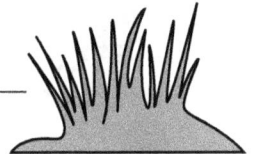

_____

_____

* **Actions speak louder than words**

_____

_____

* **A Bird in the hand is worth two in the bush**

_____

_____

* **A man is known by the company he keeps**

_____

_____

_____

MY PERFECT DAY

What would a perfect day be like for you? Where would you go; what would you do; who would you spend it with? Create the most perfect day you can imagine, and with as much detail as possible, write about it below. If you run out of room, use the back of this paper.

_____
_____
_____
_____
_____
_____
_____
_____
_____
_____
_____
_____
_____
_____
_____
_____
_____
_____

Is There Really a Perfect Person?

Write a story about a perfect person. What would this perfect person look like, who would his or her friends be, where would he or she live, what would this perfect person do for fun, and what would others think of this perfect person?

Describe this perfect person in every way you can.

_____

_____

_____

_____

_____

_____

_____

_____

_____

_____

_____

_____

_____

_____

_____

_____

_____

_____

Do you think it's possible for anyone to ever really be perfect?

Picture This

Do you know that you are a creative person? Creativity is an attitude.
It's a way of thinking about yourself and the world with a sense of
wonder. It's a way of seeing things. Creativity is expressing yourself
in your own special and unique way.

Express yourself! Turn the shapes below into your own drawings. Be
imaginative and have fun!

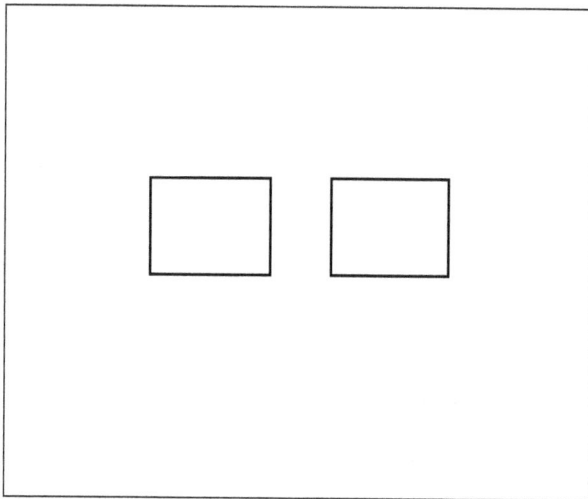

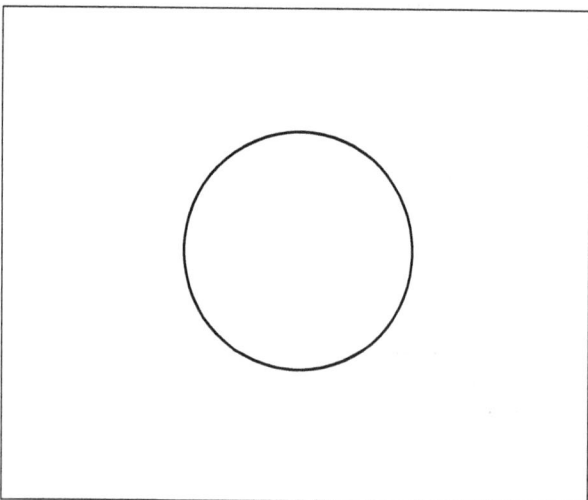

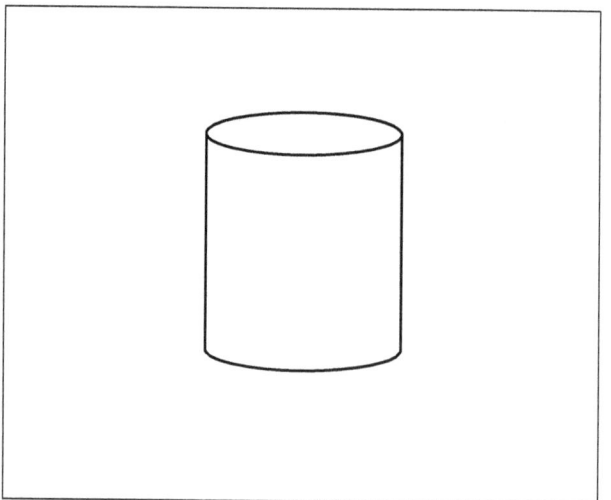

**Now trace your hand on the back of this paper. Use the outline of
your hand to draw another picture.**

Uniquely Created By ME

Creative people look at ordinary things in special ways. They see possibilities that other people might not see. Practice looking at things creatively by doing the exercises below.

Connect these dots to make a pattern or picture. Add more dots and lines. Fill in spaces and use colors if you like. Your result can be realistic or fanciful. It can be anything you like. Just practice being creative.

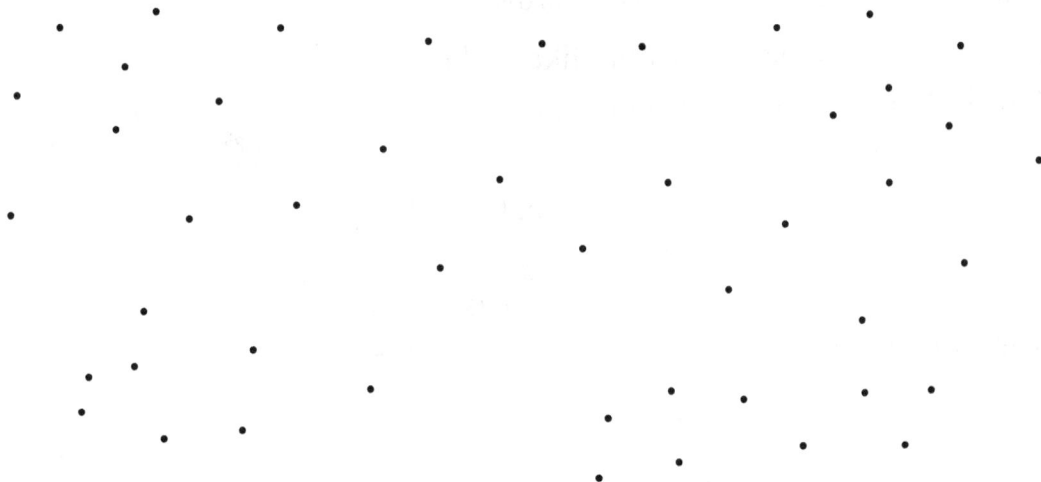

List as many uses as you can think of for each of the following items. Think of ordinary as well as unusual uses.

Water glass	Pillow	Shoe box	Clothes hanger

Create an Ideal Creature

Have you ever wished you could fly next to a seagull or swim with a dolphin?

Have you ever wanted to have arms come out of your waist when it's your turn to bat?

Have you ever wished you could send up a set of periscope eyes to see over a crowd?

Think about things that you would like to do better. Then think about special things that animals can do.

Now, create an IDEAL CREATURE that has all the best features you can imagine.

List the features here.

List the advantages of the features here.

_____   _____
_____   _____
_____   _____
_____   _____
_____   _____
_____   _____

On the back of this page draw a picture of your . . .

IDEAL CREATURE

Give your creature a name.

_____

WHO WOULD YOU LIKE TO BE?

Would you rather be

     …a famous artist? _____

     …a popular musician? _____

     …a published author? _____

     …a star athlete? _____

     …an award winning actor? _____

     …or an elected politician? _____

Put a check (✓) beside the career that appeals to you most.

In the space below write about why you picked what you did.

What have you learned about yourself from what you wrote?

_____

_____

_____

_____

Positive SELF-TALK

Do you know that the way people talk to themselves influences how they feel about themselves? Put-downs or negative self-talk can make you unhappy and discouraged, and can cause you to lose your self-confidence. So even when discouraging things happen, make sure your self-talk is positive. Positive self-talk helps you feel better and gives you the power to handle negative situations.

The kids in the pictures below are using negative self-talk. Think about how they are harming themselves. Draw new pictures that show each kid using positive self-talk. Write in the exact words each kid is saying. And remember to use positive self-talk in your life, too.

ANOTHER "F"! I'M NO GOOD AT TAKING TESTS.

I'M SO CLUMSY! I ALWAYS BREAK SOMETHING.

I'M GOING TO STRIKE OUT. I'M A LOUSY PLAYER.

My Three Wishes

1. _____

_____

_____

2. _____

_____

_____

3. _____

_____

Pretend you have found a magic lantern. If you rub it, a genie will come out and grant you three wishes. One wish is for you. One wish is for another person, and one wish is to make the world a better place.

What are your wishes?

Find the HAPPY Words

Look through the dictionary and try to find a positive word for each letter of the alphabet. Keep this list and put a check mark beside each word you use, every time you use it. Try to get at least one check beside each word.

A _____   N _____

B _____   O _____

C _____   P _____

D _____   Q _____

E _____   R _____

F _____   S _____

G _____   T _____

H _____   U _____

I _____   V _____

J _____   W _____

K _____   X _____

L _____   Y _____

M _____   Z _____

Positive Word Search

The words we use when we talk to others and when we talk to ourselves are very important. When we use positive and uplifting words, they have a good effect on us and others. When we use negative or put-down words, they have a bad effect. Be a winner. Use lots of positive words and use them often.

In the word puzzle below, there are 16 positive words plus 3 example words. They are hidden among the letters you see, and the examples show you how to find them. Draw a circle around each word.

f	r	i	c	h	z	b	a	r	s	u	x	d	c	b	t
y	e	x	c	e	l	l	e	n	t	a	n	i	c	e	a
s	t	e	e	i	o	o	x	y	m	n	a	c	v	d	b
i	s	t	u	p	u	v	s	g	o	x	k	i	n	d	t
i	h	u	v	p	a	e	z	o	s	j	g	k	e	k	s
m	a	l	p	l	y	l	q	o	x	a	r	g	a	r	t
y	r	u	n	e	e	t	v	d	u	u	e	w	t	f	h
a	e	i	o	a	r	w	u	c	t	h	a	n	k	s	p
b	t	z	o	s	m	o	r	t	z	i	t	a	k	y	d
c	s	u	p	e	r	i	o	r	r	a	f	g	u	s	e
j	o	y	i	p	t	q	w	a	z	h	a	p	p	y	z
z	b	c	a	t	s	x	a	o	v	l	x	a	e	t	s

Word Box

excellent	happy	nice	super
give	joy	please	superior
good	kind	proud	thanks
great	love	share	yes

Now do this: On another sheet of paper put each of the positive words in a sentence. See how many of these words you can use today.

What Do They Mean?

Unscramble each of the words below and then look up its definition and write it in the space below the word.

FOYJUL _____
Correct Word

Definition _____
_____

PSINERI _____
Correct Word

Definition _____
_____

CESCUSS _____
Correct Word

Definition _____
_____

PTORPUS _____
Correct Word

Definition _____
_____

AGEROUCNE _____
Correct Word

Definition _____
_____

CSIDRVEO _____
Correct Word

Definition _____
_____

INDFRELY _____
Correct Word

Definition _____
_____

CISPEAL _____
Correct Word

Definition _____
_____

Taking Care of Me!

There are many things you can do to take good care of yourself. Think about the things on this sheet, and try to do them for yourself.

Eat Right. Don't skip breakfast. Cut down on sweets. Eat lots of healthy foods like fresh fruits and vegetables. List 4 healthy foods that you like to eat:

1. _____   3. _____

2. _____   4. _____

Laugh! Tell a joke. Make a funny face. Draw your funny face on the back of this page.

Exercise! List 3 ways YOU can get regular exercise:

1. _____

2. _____

3. _____

Voice your feelings! When something's bothering you, to whom can you talk?_____

Take action on your problems! Do you have a problem right now? What can you do to solve it? _____

_____

_____

If you can't solve the problem, change your feelings! It helps to remember this motto: *If you don't get what you want, want what you get.*

Organize! Make good use of your time. Get your work done. What can you do to be better organized?_____

_____

_____

Relax! Breath deeply. Get lots of sleep. Eat right, exercise and think positive thoughts, and you'll be taking good care of yourself.

Special People!

Think of the people who are special to you. These are people you really care about and look forward to seeing. You would miss them if they weren't around. Write your name on the line in the center of the star, and on the lines at each of the star points write the name of a special person in your life.

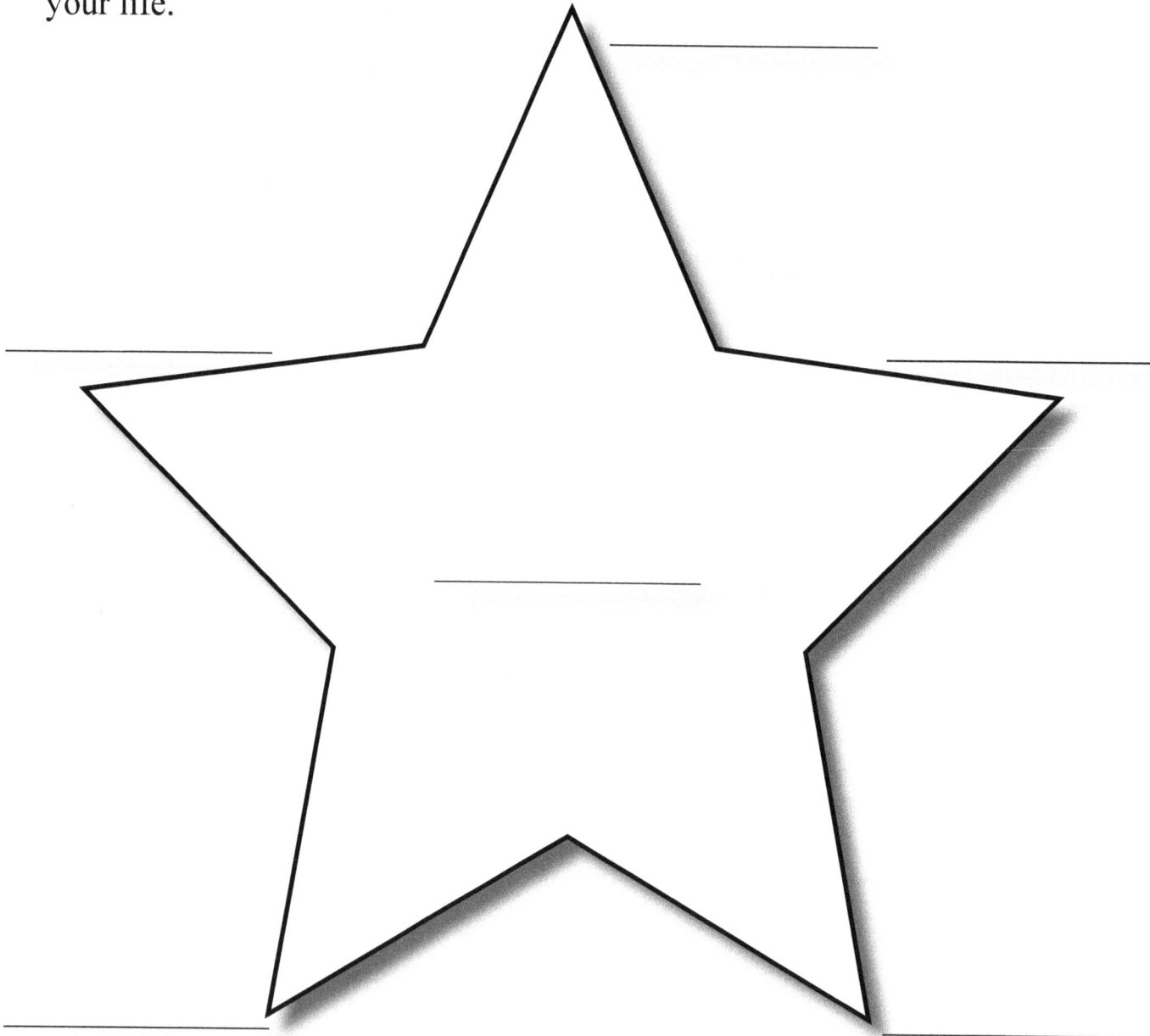

Inside each point of the star, write why that person is special to you.

FRIENDSHIP

A friend is a present you give yourself
—Robert Louis Stevenson

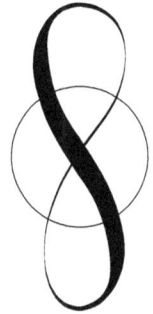

Friends are very important to all of us.
Friendship means giving, sharing, and caring.

These are things I value in a friend:

_____

_____

_____

These are some things I like to do with my friends:

_____

_____

_____

Something nice a friend did for me was:

_____

_____

_____

Here are some things I can do to make friends:

_____

_____

_____

This is one way I can show that I'm a good friend:

_____

_____

_____

_____

A SECRET MESSAGE
to a Friend

In 1835, Samuel Morse invented the telegraph and soon afterward, invented the Morse Code. Morse Code is made up of dots and dashes that are combined to stand for the letters of the alphabet, numbers and even punctuation. To use Morse Code the person sending a message tapped out the dots and dashes on a telegraph machine. The telegraph machine receiving the message made the short sounds of dots and the long sounds of dashes. When this invention was used, it was the first time in history that people could communicate over long distances.

Try sending a message in Morse Code to a friend. Use the Morse Code below to write your message.

A •—	J •———	S •••	0 —————	
B —•••	K —•—	T —	1 •————	
C —•—•	L •—••	U ••—	2 ••———	
D —••	M ——	V •••—	3 •••——	period •—•—•—
E •	N —•	W •——	4 ••••—	comma ——••——
F ••—•	O ———	X —••—	5 •••••	colon ———•••
G ——•	P •——•	Y —•——	6 —••••	question mark ••——••
H ••••	Q ——•—	Z ——••	7 ——•••	apostrophe •————•
I ••	R •—•		8 ———••	quotation marks •—••—•
			9 ————•	

Here is a sample message so that you can see how a message is written. Notice how a | is used to separate the letters in each word. || is used to separate each word, number or punctuation mark. Here is the sample message:

Friends are important people.

•• — • | • — • | •• | • | — • | — •• | ••• || • — | • — • | • ||
•• | — — | • — — • | — — — | • — • | — | • — | — • | — ||
• — — • | • | — — — | • — — • | • — •• | • || • — • — • —

MORE

48

Now here's a special message for you. Decode the message and see what it says.

— •— — | — — — | ••— ‖ •— | •— • | • ‖ •— ‖
— — • | •— • | • | •— | — ‖ — •— | •• | — •• ‖ •— •— •—

Now try sending a special message to one of your friends. Use the following form and write on the lines in Morse Code.

Dear _____

    Something I like about you is _____

_____

_____

_____

_____

_____

_____

_____

_____

    Your friend _____

My Circle of Friends

We all have friends
and know how important friends are.
Write the names of your friends on the lines
around YOUR circle of friends below.

Draw a picture of yourself on the
figure without a face. Then, draw a circle around each
word that describes your friends. Draw a line from each
word to the friend or friends that word describes.

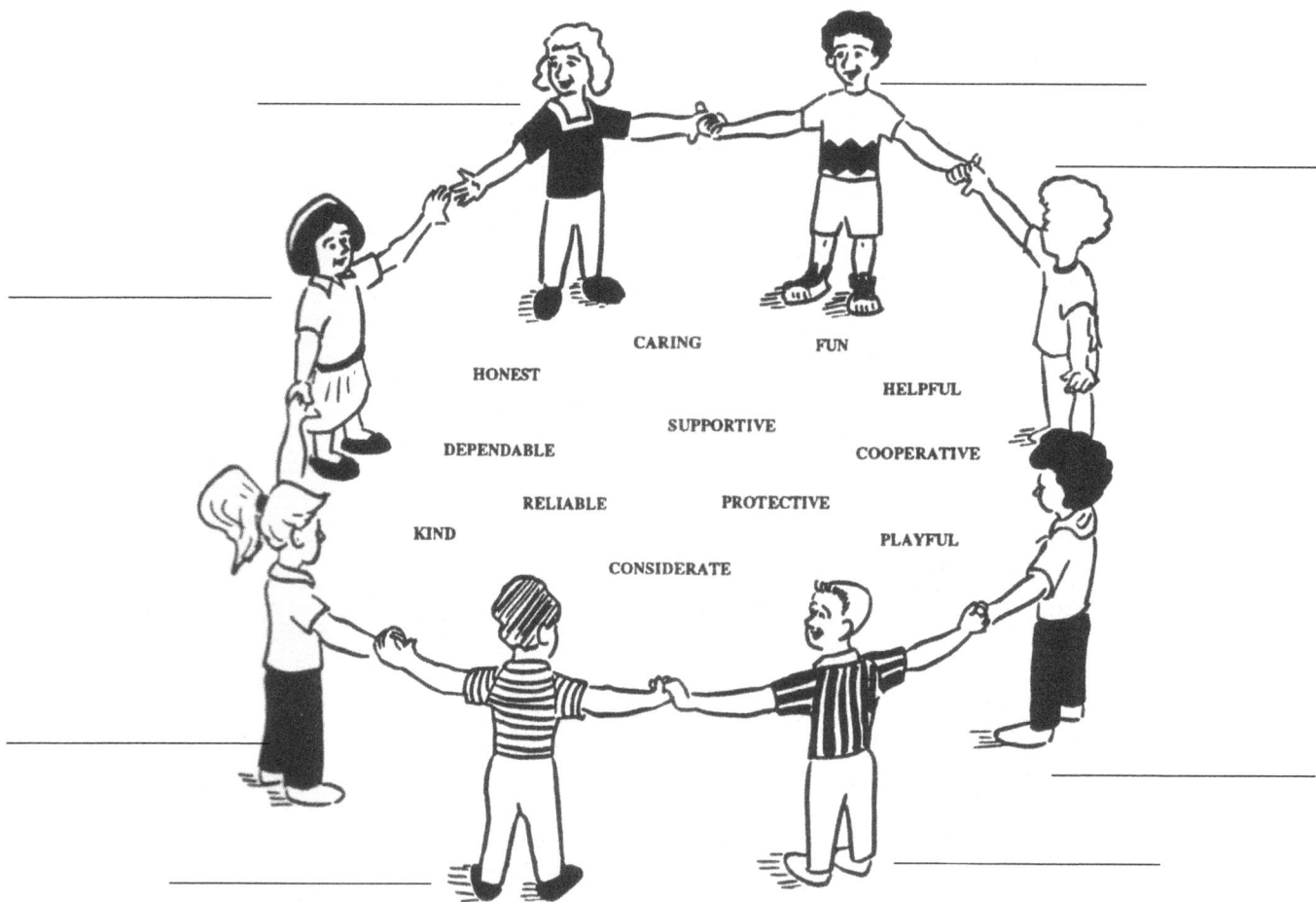

CARING   FUN

HONEST   HELPFUL

SUPPORTIVE

DEPENDABLE   COOPERATIVE

RELIABLE   PROTECTIVE

KIND   PLAYFUL

CONSIDERATE

TALKING KINDLY TO OTHERS

The things you say to others can make them feel certain ways. Unkind words can cause hurt feelings. Pleasant and kind words help others to feel good and help them to treat others kindly, too. What good thoughts and kind actions directed toward others can you write about on the hearts below?

FRIENDLY Deeds

A friendly deed is something you do to help another person or to make someone else feel good. You might help a neighbor by carrying her groceries into her house, or you could say something nice that made someone smile.

Describe a friendly deed that you have done to help someone or to make someone feel good.

_____

_____

_____

_____

_____

_____

_____

How did you feel about yourself when you did the friendly deed?

_____

_____

Why do you think it's important to try to do friendly deeds whenever possible?

_____

_____

_____

_____

_____

Being KIND

Shall we make a new rule of life from tonight;
always try to be a little kinder than is necessary.

J.M. Barrie, *Peter Pan*

Think of a kind act that you can do today. Describe the kind act here:

_____

_____

_____

Draw a picture of you doing the kind act.

Now, go do the kind act and then write one word that describes how you feel.

_____

The Pleasure of Gift Giving

Giving a gift to someone is a wonderful thing to do. Gifts make the receiver feel happy, and the giver also has a good feeling. Giving really special gifts to others takes some thinking and knowing something about what the receiver needs or wants. Pick five people in your life, and write their names on the gift tags. Then, in the boxes, describe what the gift is. Remember, your gift can be anything, from something material like a new car to something intangible like love or friendship.

GIVING THANKS

Everyone has things they are thankful for. Some are big important things and others are simple everyday kinds of things. What's important is to be thankful and to take time every day to give thanks for all you do have.

What are you thankful for? List everything you can think of. Add to the list as more things come to mind.

_____ _____ _____

_____ _____ _____

_____ _____ _____

_____ _____ _____

_____ _____ _____

_____ _____ _____

_____ _____ _____

_____ _____ _____

_____ _____ _____

_____ _____ _____

_____ _____ _____

_____ _____ _____

Have Your Ever Felt   Left Out?

Fill in the bubbles with the words you think the kids are thinking and saying.

Have you ever been left out?_____

How did you feel?_____

What do you think is happening in the picture? _____

_____

_____

If you were one of this group of kids, what could you do to
make the girl feel included?_____

_____

_____

A Famous Person

If you could meet one famous person in history, who would he or she be? _____

What is it about this person that makes him or her interesting to you?

_____

_____

_____

_____

_____

_____

Use the internet and look up your famous person. **Write a brief biography of the person. Highlight the things you most admire.**

_____

_____

_____

_____

_____

_____

_____

_____

_____

_____

_____

A Treasure Hunt for People

Every person is a treasure. Discover some of the treasures in others by finding three people to fit each category below. Have each person write his or her name on a line in the correct box.

I found a person WHO...

Has been to Disneyland or Disneyworld.

1. _____
2. _____
3. _____

Has Pizza as a favorite food.

1. _____
2. _____
3. _____

Has a hobby.

1. _____ **The hobby is:**
2. _____ **The hobby is:**
3. _____ **The hobby is:**

Has travelled outside the United States.

1. _____
2. _____
3. _____

There is more treasure on the next page –

Here are some more treasures –

Wants to go to college.

1. _____
2. _____
3. _____

Owns a pet.

1. _____ The pet is a: _____
2. _____ The pet is a: _____
3. _____ The pet is a: _____

Is the oldest in the family.

1. _____
2. _____
3. _____

Has blue as a favorite color.

1. _____
2. _____
3. _____

Walks to school.

1. _____
2. _____
3. _____

Knows how to swim.

1. _____
2. _____
3. _____

Has won a prize.

1. _____ A prize for: _____
2. _____ A prize for: _____
3. _____ A prize for: _____

One of the Best Times I've Had with My Family

What are some of the things you like to do with your family? Do you enjoy big holiday meals together, or do you take family vacations? Do you go to church together, or the movies, or to a park or beach? How about celebrating birthdays or spending quiet times together? Think about one of the **BEST TIMES** you've had with your family and write about it here:

_____

_____

_____

_____

_____

_____

_____

_____

_____

_____

My Family Tree

You are a unique and special person with many wonderful qualities and traits. Some of these qualities and traits you've inherited or learned from your family. So one way to get better acquainted with yourself is to find out more about your family.

Begin by taking a look at your family heritage ("roots"). Fill in the blanks on the family tree with as many names as you can. Ask another family member for help if you need it. If you find out the names of relatives who go back even farther, write as many as you can in the top of the tree.

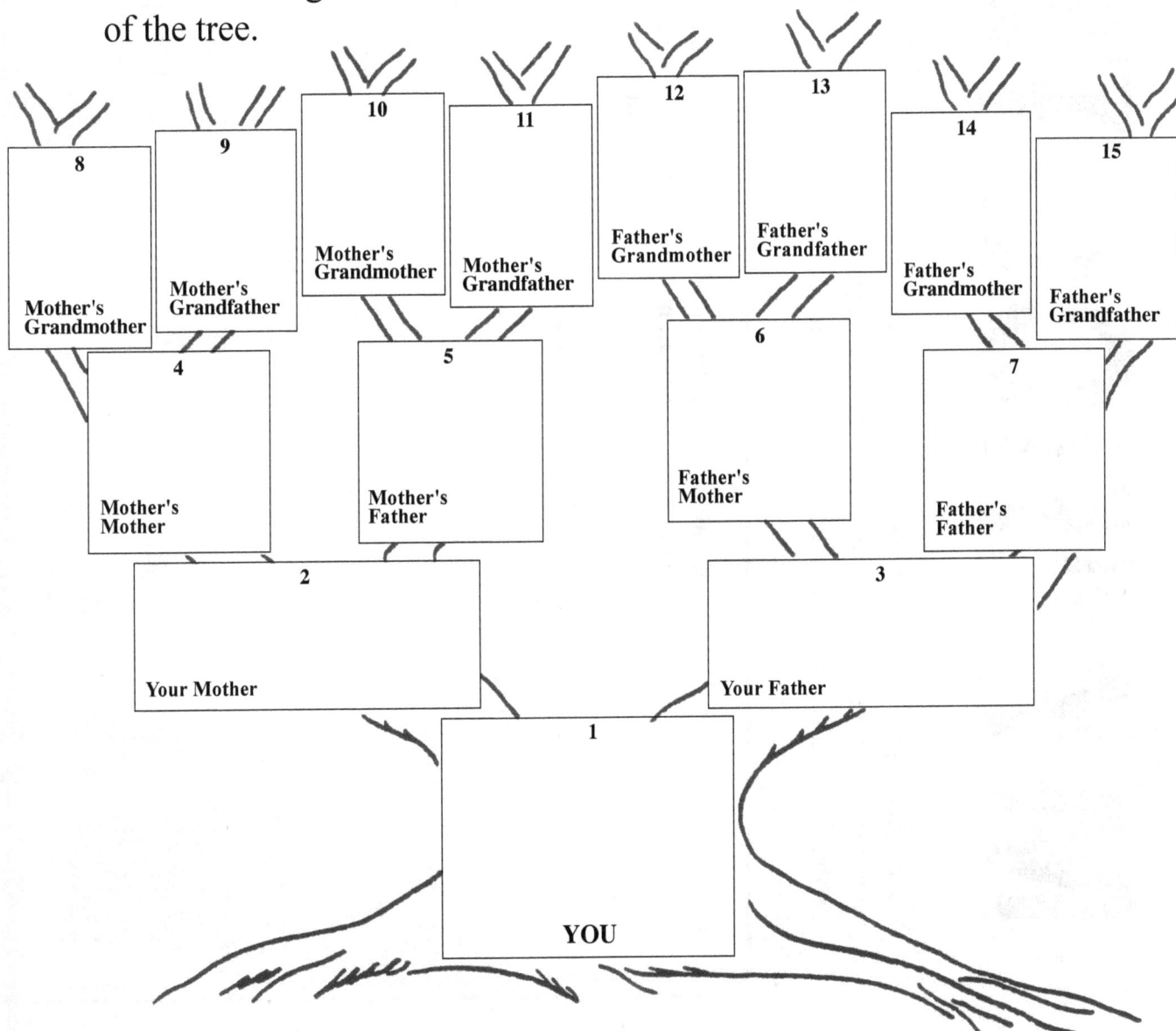

8
Mother's Grandmother

9
Mother's Grandfather

10
Mother's Grandmother

11
Mother's Grandfather

12
Father's Grandmother

13
Father's Grandfather

14
Father's Grandmother

15
Father's Grandfather

4
Mother's Mother

5
Mother's Father

6
Father's Mother

7
Father's Father

2
Your Mother

3
Your Father

1
YOU

MY "ROOTS" ... 1

Now that you've done your family tree, investigate your roots even further. Write down the names of all of the relatives listed on your family tree. Then fill in the information about each one. To complete this chart, you'll probably need the help of an adult family member.

Name of relative	Relationship to me	Race, ethnicity, or nationality	Where did this relative live most of his or her life?	Occupation	Memorable things about him or her
1. ME •••					
2.					
3.					
4.					
5.					
6.					
7.					
8.					

MY "ROOTS" ... 2

Name of relative	Relationship to you	Race, ethnicity, or nationality	Where did this relative live most of his or her life?	Occupation	Memorable things about him or her
9.					
10.					
11.					
12.					
13.					
14.					
15.					

What have you learned about your ancestors from doing this chart? _____

What have you learned about your family? _____

What have you learned about yourself? _____

WHAT WOULD YOU TELL YOUR CHILDREN?

Imagine that you are a parent, and that you have a son and a daughter your age. What important message would you give each of them? Write the messages below.

To my daughter:

_____
_____
_____
_____
_____
_____
_____
_____

To my son:

_____
_____
_____
_____
_____
_____
_____

Fear Is a MONSTER

Think about times when you were afraid of someone or something, but then everything turned out okay. Just as monsters aren't real, most of the time our fears aren't real either. Think of it this way:

FEAR = **F**alse **E**vidence **A**ppearing **R**eal

In the left-hand column, write about fears you have had. In the right-hand column, write about what really happened.

My FEAR:

What really happened:

_____   _____

_____   _____

_____   _____

_____   _____

_____   _____

Rules are Rules

Think of the many different areas of your life in which you are required to follow the rules. Then answer these questions:

The best rule at home is: _____

_____

The worst rule at school is: _____

_____

It should be changed because: _____

_____

_____

If I were in charge of the world, here are three rules I would make immediately:

Rule: _____

Reason for rule: _____

_____

Rule: _____

Reason for rule: _____

_____

Rule: _____

Reason for rule: _____

_____

_____

Get Ready for a . . .
Great Career!

It's not too early to start thinking about your dream job. Here's one good way to start: List four things you really like to do. Make sure they are fun things that interest you a lot.

1. _____   2. _____

3. _____   4. _____

Good for you! Now go back and read each thing you wrote down. Draw a circle around each thing that you are good at—or are showing improvement in.

Did you know you could have a job someday doing one or more of the things you listed? Ask your friends to help you brainstorm careers that relate to the things you listed and circled. Write your ideas here:

1. _____

2. _____

3. _____

4. _____

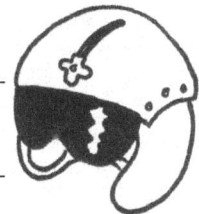

Play detective! Here are some questions to ask that will help you find out how adults with great careers got where they are today:

1. *Do you like your job?*
2. *When did you first start to consider going into this career?*
3. *Do you do anything in your job that you were doing when you were my age?*
4. *How did you prepare for this career?*
5. *What has been the secret of your success?*

Jumping to the Wrong Conclusion

Have you ever jumped to the wrong conclusion about an event or situation? This means that before you took the time to think carefully about what was happening, you just immediately made a judgment that turned out not to be correct.

Write about a time when you jumped to the wrong conclusion.

_____

_____

_____

_____

_____

_____

_____

_____

_____

_____

_____

_____

_____

_____

_____

_____

Drawing the Right Conclusion

Now consider the event about which you jumped to the wrong conclusion, but take time to think it through, and consider all the possibilities.

Write a new ending and this time base it on more accurate information and thoughtful consideration.

_____

_____

_____

_____

_____

_____

_____

_____

_____

_____

_____

_____

_____

An ACCOMPLISHMENT I'm Proud Of

We accomplish things every day. Most of the time we don't stop to think about our accomplishments or acknowledge ourselves for our achievements. Things we do for ourselves and others are accomplishments that we can be proud of and feel good about. Think about an accomplishment you're proud of and write about it here.

My accomplishment was:

_____

_____

_____

_____

I achieved it by:

_____

_____

_____

_____

My accomplishment made me feel:

_____

_____

_____

_____

Attitude Makes the Difference

Have you ever noticed that when you have a bad attitude about a situation things don't seem to go so well for you? On the other hand, when you have a good attitude things seem to work out well.

What color do you think represents a bad attitude? _____

Draw a picture of a bad attitude using only the "bad attitude" color.

What color do you think represents a good attitude? _____

Draw a picture of a good attitude using only the "good attitude" color.

Think of a time that your bad attitude ruined something for you—**Now write a story about how the bad situation might have turned out better if you'd had a good attitude about the situation. Use more paper if you need it.**

_____

_____

_____

_____

_____

Success Behaviors

Read the list of eight short sentences below. Each sentence states a very important success behavior. People who *make it a habit* to do these things are almost always successful. If you make it a habit to do these things at school, there's no puzzle about it—you will be successful.

BE POSITIVE.
COMPLETE ALL WORK ASSIGNED.
BE HONEST.
BE ON TIME.

HELP OTHERS.
DO THE BEST JOB I CAN.
COOPERATE WITH OTHERS.
BE FRIENDLY.

Fill in the blank spaces below with the letters that will complete a sentence from the list above. Some letters are already there. Use them as clues to help you complete this word puzzle.

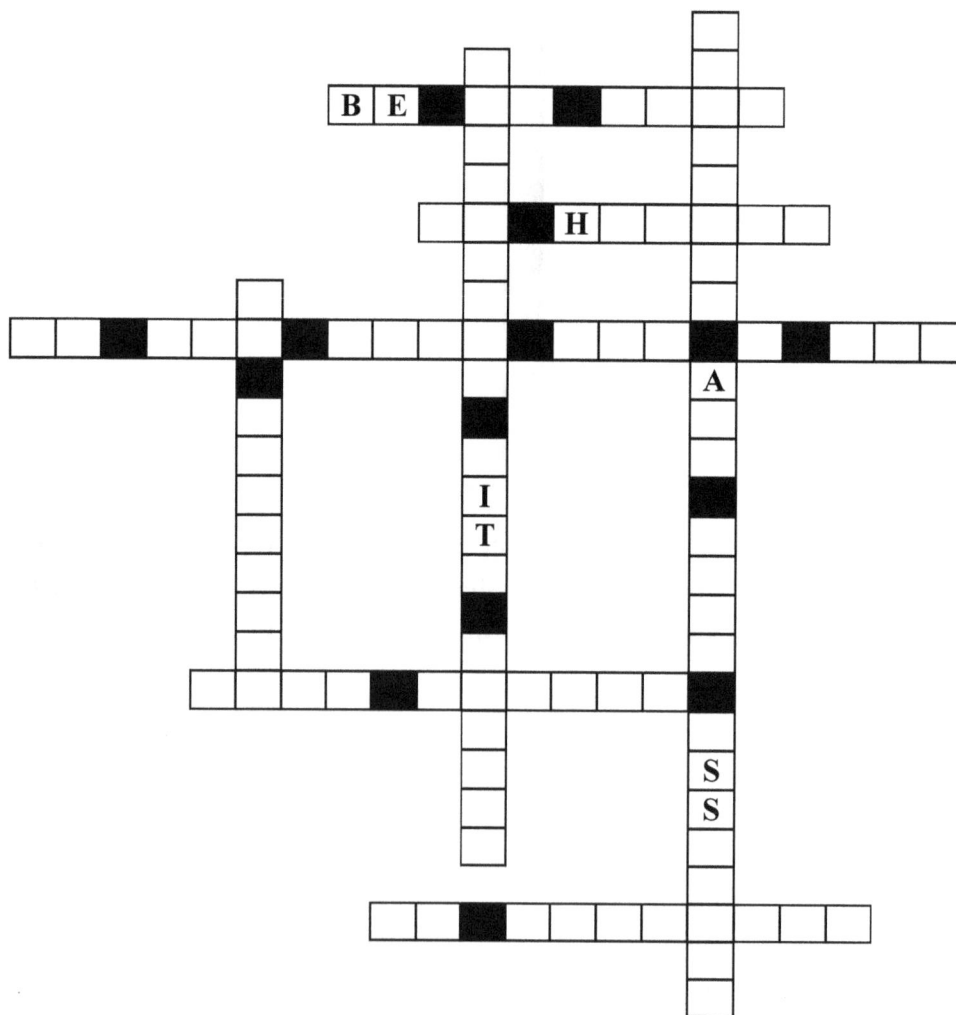

THE DREAM WITHIN

Champions aren't made in gyms. Champions are made from something they have deep inside them—a desire, a dream, a vision.

Muhammad Ali

Do you have a deep desire, a dream of something you would like to do or become someday?

Write about your dream with as much detail as you can. Also, write about how you will feel when you achieve your dream.

_____

_____

_____

_____

_____

_____

_____

_____

_____

_____

_____

_____

On another sheet of paper draw a picture of you achieving your dream.

NOTE . . .

The following skill building activity sheets are grouped into three areas. Within each group, the activities are designed to be sequential and developmental. There are eight (8) sequential activities for problem solving, six (6) sequential activities in decision making and seven (7) sequential activities in goal setting. You may choose to provide a sequential area all at once or spread the activities in that area over several lessons.

To enhance the understanding of the children relative to each area, it is recommended that you discuss each activity sheet and elaborate on what it is requesting children to think and write about. When the children finish with the sheet, involve them in discussion concerning what they are learning and how they can apply this in their lives.

Steps for Solving a PROBLEM

Problems are something that everyone has. Problems are a part of life. Sometimes people try to ignore problems and hope that they will go away. But, that's not what usually happens. Most of the time, if you ignore a problem, it just gets worse. Remember, there's nothing wrong with you if you have a problem. The important thing is to solve your problems as well as you can.

The following seven "Steps For Solving A Problem" are used by successful and happy people. Try this process when you have a problem and see how it helps you.

1. Decide if the problem is really yours. Could it be someone else's?

2. Know exactly what the problem is.

3. Do you need to get help?

4. Think of ALL the ways you could solve the problem.

5. Consider the possible consequences of each idea for solving the problem.

6. Make a decision.

7. Follow through on the decision.

**Now let's take a look at each
step in more detail.**

STEP 1 *Is It Really MY Problem?*

Think about a problem that you have. If the problem bothering you is really someone else's, let that person solve it.

Do you agree that people have to solve their own problems? _____

What can happen if people try to solve other people's problems and ignore their own?

_____

_____

_____

_____

_____

If it is your problem, don't blame someone else for causing it. That won't work either. Say to yourself: This is my problem, and I will do my best to solve it.

Do you agree that it doesn't help to blame someone else for causing a problem that is yours?_____

Have you ever had someone blame you for causing his or her problem?_____

Did blaming you help that person solve the problem?

_____

_____

_____

2 *Name the Problem*

Knowing exactly what the problem is helps a lot. Try not to be confused by it. Writing down a description of the problem can help you understand it.

Name your problem here:

_____

_____

_____

_____

_____

Describe your problem here:

_____

_____

_____

_____

_____

_____

_____

_____

_____

STEP 3 Do I Need HELP?

People who care about you are usually happy to offer assistance when you ask them for help. But don't try to get a helper to solve your problem for you. Ask the helper to listen and make suggestions.

_____ 1. Yes, I'd like help from someone who cares about me.

_____ 2. No. I think I'd better solve this problem on my own.

If you checked 1, list the names of people with whom you could talk about your problem:

_____

_____

_____

_____

_____

_____

_____

4 How Many Ways Can I Solve the Problem

Ask yourself: What are some things I can do to solve my problem? It's a good idea to write down all the ideas you come up with. That way you won't forget any of them.

Write down your ideas about the things you can do to solve your problem:

1. _____
_____
_____

2. _____
_____
_____

3. _____
_____
_____

4. _____
_____
_____

5. _____
_____
_____

Use another sheet of paper if you need to write down more ideas.

STEP 5

The Consequences of Each Idea

Carefully think over each idea you came up with in Step 4. For each idea ask yourself: What will happen to me and the other people involved if I try this idea?

Write down the consequences of each idea:

1. _____
   _____
   _____

2. _____
   _____
   _____

3. _____
   _____
   _____

4. _____
   _____
   _____

5. _____
   _____
   _____

Use another sheet of paper if you need to write down more consequences.

6 Decide What to Do

Go ahead and make a decision. If you have done all the steps before this one, your decision will probably be a good one. It may not be easy to do, but it stands a good chance of working.

Once again, state your problem here:

_____

_____

_____

_____

_____

Now describe what you are going to do to solve the problem:

_____

_____

_____

_____

_____

STEP 7 Stick to the Decision

Once you decide what to do, give your decision a chance. Go with it for awhile to see if it is really the best solution. Remember, if it doesn't work, or causes more problems, don't blame yourself. You did the best you could. Just start over again with the steps for solving a problem.

Now that you've gone through the 7-step process for solving problems, what have you learned about problem solving?

_____

_____

_____

Were these steps helpful to you? _____

Remember, you can use this process for the rest of your life. How do you feel about yourself now that you've learned a way to attack any problem you run up against?

_____

_____

_____

_____

_____

_____

_____

END

The DECISION-MAKING Process

Whether you realize it, you are always making decisions. Every day you make lots of little decisions, like what to wear to school, what to watch on T.V., whom to play with at recess, and more.

What are some little decisions you've already made today?

_____

_____

_____

_____

_____

Sometimes you make big decisions too, like how to spend your summer vacation, or whether to talk to someone about a problem you're having. **What is one big decision you have made?**

_____

_____

_____

You'll be making decisions throughout your entire life. While you are learning and growing, you may not feel comfortable making extremely important decisions. Gradually it will get easier— especially if you learn the following 5-step process for decision making.

STEP
1

State the Decision To Be Made

The first step in making sound decisions is to clearly state the decision to be made. In the space below, describe a decision that you must make:

_____

_____

_____

_____

_____

_____

_____

_____

2 Know What's Important and What You Really Want

Decisions are made in order to reach a desired goal—to have or do something you want. Think about what you really want to have or to have happen.

In the space below write about your goals in as much detail as possible:

_____

_____

_____

_____

_____

_____

_____

_____

3 Gather Information

Have you ever heard the term "informed decision?" It means the decision is based on facts and thought. It is a decision made with the benefit of INFORMATION. For you to make an informed decision, you need to gather information—as much of it as you can get. The more information you have, the better your chances of making a wise decision. To gather information you can talk to people, ask questions, read, watch television, use the internet, and make observations. Do whatever is necessary to get the information you need.

List here the people you'll talk to and what you'll do to get information:

_____

_____

_____

_____

_____

On the back of this sheet, write notes to yourself about the information and facts you gather.

4 Find and List Alternatives

Now that you have gathered lots of information, think about all the choices (alternatives) you have. Understanding the advantages and disadvantages of each alternative will help you make the best decision.

On the chart below, list the alternatives you have in making your decision. Then, list the advantages and disadvantages of each.

Alternative	Advantages	Disadvantages

Now look at each alternative and ask yourself: What will happen to me and to the other people involved if I choose this alternative?

5 Make A Decision

Now that you've described the decision that must be made, looked at what's important to you, gathered information, and listed your alternatives, go ahead and make a decision.

Write about your final decision here:

_____

_____

_____

_____

_____

_____

_____

_____

_____

_____

Develop a plan for putting your decision into action. The goal-setting process that follows will help you do that.

END

I CAN BECAUSE
I THINK I CAN

Read the title of this activity sheet. What does it mean to you? When there is something you really want to do and you believe you can do it, then make it a goal. YOU CAN DO IT!

Think about the things you'd like to do during the coming year.

Complete each of the sentences below:

1. I want to learn to _____

_____

_____

2. I want to read _____

_____

_____

3. I want to make _____

_____

_____

4. I want to visit _____

_____

_____

Now look at the steps for achieving all these things.

1 All the Things I'd Like To Do

When you want to work on goal setting, start by making a list of things you would like to do. Write down things you'd like to learn and things you'd like to do better. List things you want to buy, places you want to go, books you want to read, or anything at all. Don't worry about how to achieve your goals, just make a list.

1. _____

2. _____

3. _____

4. _____

5. _____

6. _____

7. _____

8. _____

9. _____

10. _____

Use more paper if you need to.

2 Setting a GOAL

Step two is to select ONE special goal to start work on now.

My Goal –

_____

_____

_____

_____

_____

Set the date by which you want to achieve your goal.

I want to achieve my goal by _____

Think about why you want to achieve this goal. List as many reasons as you can think of here:

1. _____

2. _____

3. _____

4. _____

5. _____

6. _____

Read this list often to stay interested in your goal. If you keep thinking about why you want to reach your goal, you'll work to get there.

3 Steps to Reaching MY Goal

In order to actually reach your goal, there are things you need to do. On another piece of paper write down everything you can think of that you need to do to get to your goal. List things like who you can ask for help, information you need to get, skills you need to learn, money you need to earn, etc.

After you've written every step you can think of, write them down on this sheet in the order you plan to do them.

1. _____
2. _____
3. _____
4. _____
5. _____
6. _____
7. _____
8. _____
9. _____
10. _____

As you work toward your goal, you may become aware of more steps you need to take. Add them to this list. Use the other side of this sheet if you need to.

4 PEP Talk to Myself

Sometimes achieving a goal becomes a difficult task. If you feel like giving up on your goal, what are some things to remember that pep you up?

_____

_____

_____

_____

_____

What are some things that might stop you from reaching your goal?	What can you do to prevent these things from stopping you?
1.	
2.	
3.	
4.	

5 A Picture of My Goal

One helpful thing you can do to reach your goal is to get a clear mental picture of what you want to achieve. In the space below, draw a picture of you achieving your goal. Or paste in pictures from magazines that help you see your goal more clearly.

Stay on track. Keep this picture in your mind. Think about it often and you'll find yourself getting closer to your goal.

6 I Have Reached My Goal!

CONGRATULATIONS!

Now that you've reached your goal, how do you feel?

_____

_____

_____

What did you learn about goal setting?

_____

_____

_____

What did you learn about yourself?

_____

_____

_____

It's time to start thinking about your next goal!

END

If your heart is in Social-Emotional
Learning, visit us online.

Come see us at
www.InnerchoicePublishing.com

Our web site gives you a look at all our other Social-Emotional
Learning-based books, free activities, articles, research, and
learning and teaching strategies. Every week you'll get a new
Sharing Circle topic and lesson.

INNERCHOICE Publishing
15079 Oak Chase Court
Wellington, FL 33414

www.ingramcontent.com/pod-product-compliance
Lightning Source LLC
Chambersburg PA
CBHW062032090426
42733CB00034B/2590